Allen Iverson

Motion & Emotion

By

Mark Stewart

THE MILLBROOK PRESS
BROOKFIELD, CONNECTICUT

M

THE MILLBROOK PRESS

Produced by
BITTERSWEET PUBLISHING
John Sammis, President
and
TEAM STEWART, INC.
RESEARCHED AND EDITED BY MIKE KENNEDY

Series Design and Electronic Page Makeup by
JAFFE ENTERPRISES
Ron Jaffe

All photos courtesy AP/ Wide World Photos, Inc. except the following:
Craig Jones/Allsport — Cover
Newport News Daily Press — Pages 6, 8, 10, 11, 12, 15, 16
The following images are from the collection of Team Stewart:
Topps, Inc. — Page 17 (© 1968)
USA World University Games — Page 23
Beckett Future Stars — Page 27 (© 1996)
Topps, Inc. — Page 32 (©1978)
Time, Inc. — Page 42 (© 1999)

Printed in the United States of America

Published by
The Millbrook Press, Inc.
2 Old New Milford Road
Brookfield, Connecticut   06804

www.millbrookpress.com

Library of Congress Cataloging-in-Publication Data

Stewart, Mark.
   Allen Iverson: motion & emotion / by Mark Stewart
   p.   cm.   — (Basketball's new wave)
   Includes index.
   ISBN 0-7613-1958-1 (lib. bdg.)
   1. Iverson, Allen, 1975– —Juvenile literature. 2. Basketball players—United States—Biography—
Juvenile literature. [1. Iverson, Allen, 1975– . 2. Basketball players.] I. Title: Motion & emotion. II.
Title. III. Series
GV884.I84 S84 2000
796.323'092--dc21
[B]   00-040182

1 3 5 7 9 10 8 6 4 2

Contents

My Mother Made Me Do It

"I came home one day and my mom told me I was going to basketball practice."

— ALLEN IVERSON

There are many ways to take the measure of a professional basketball player. There are statistics like points, assists, steals, and rebounds. There are awards and honors. And there are million-dollar contracts and big-money commercials and endorsement deals. There also is that extra something that is often hard to put your finger on. It is a combination of things, such as the fear a player creates on the court, the excitement he generates in the arena, and the emotions he stirs among the people who watch him play. Allen Iverson scores big in each of these categories.

Allen also has a reputation. It has followed him like a shadow since he was a kid. He has been called many things, including "unpredictable" and "dangerous." Whether or not he deserves these labels—and whether or not he enjoys them—has been one of basketball's great mysteries. There is no mystery, however, about what Allen can do with a basketball in his hands. He is one of history's most mesmerizing one-man shows. The most fantastic thing about Allen is not his devastating crossover dribble, or his

With his cornrows and tattoos, Allen Iverson is one of the most recognizable athletes in the world. That is fine with him—he has felt the glare of the sports spotlight since he was a teenager.

Allen and family during his high-school years. His mother, Ann, is at left.

withering glare, or his crazy, hip-hop gangster image. No, the scariest thing about him is that he keeps getting better, and no one is quite sure how good he will one day be.

What most fans do *not* know about Allen is that, if the breaks had gone his way, he would have been doing his thing with a football, not a basketball. As far back as he or anyone else in Hampton, Virginia, can remember, Allen Iverson was the best quarterback anyone had ever seen. Allen had a great arm, incredible speed, and moves that sometimes seemed superhuman.

When Allen faded back, opponents prayed he would pass. At least then there was a chance to stop him. They did not want to see him tuck the ball under his arm and head for the goal line, because no one could bring him down. Allen loved football. There was never a moment when he felt the game was out of his control.

> "My mom and my sister, I just wanted to get them out of the projects so bad. I was just so hungry. So hungry. I was starving."
>
> **ALLEN IVERSON**

Unfortunately, the same could not be said about Allen's home life. His mother, Ann, was only 15 when he was born June 7, 1975, and Allen's father walked out on the family shortly thereafter. The man of the house for most of Allen's life was Michael Freeman, who moved in with Ann when Allen was a toddler. Ann and Michael stayed together for more than a dozen years, and had two daughters, Brandy and Iiesha.

Michael worked at a low-paying job in the shipyards and Ann did whatever odd jobs she could to pay the rent and keep food on the table. But the best they could afford was a tiny apartment in a rat-infested housing project. Sometimes there was not enough money to keep the lights on. Once, a waste pipe burst under the floor and raw sewage leaked into their apartment for more than a month before it was fixed.

Did You Know?

Allen's friends called him "Bubba-Chuck," after the names of his two uncles.

The only thing that kept Allen from giving up was the love and support of his mother. Ann Iverson kept telling her children how important they were, and that no matter how bad things looked, nothing was out of their reach if they tried hard enough. It was at this time that Allen began thinking he might become a professional athlete.

Even after discovering the joys of basketball, Allen's first love was still football.

The sport he was thinking about was still football. As far as he was concerned, basketball was for kids who were not tough enough to play football. Even though Michael loved basketball and took Allen to the park to watch pickup games, the boy would refuse to set foot on the court. The game just did not seem to have the speed, power, and strategy that football did. It seemed "soft."

Just before Allen's ninth birthday, his mother decided it was time for him to give hoops a serious try. She arranged for him to join a team, and spent her hard-earned money to make sure he had the best shoes a young player could buy. Allen knew he had to do what his mother said, but he did not have to like it. "She bought me a pair of brand-new Jordans to go in, which was good," says Allen. "But, I mean, I cried all the way out the door. She made me go—she *made* me go."

By the time Allen got home from his first practice, however, he was hooked. "When I got there," he remembers, "I saw guys on my football team, and it was fun. I came home and thanked her, and I've been playing ever since."

Sticking With It

chapter **1**

> *"I wanted to be the first Iverson to make it."*
> — **ALLEN IVERSON**

Trouble was never far away in Allen's neighborhood. High unemployment, low income, and the availability of drugs made the streets explosive. In the summers, when high temperature sent everyone outdoors, there was little else to do but hang out and get into trouble. Like many boys his age, Allen felt the pull of the streets. Had it not been for his sports, and a young man named Tony Clark, Allen might have been just another sad story.

Tony was seven years older than Allen. He saw something special in the boy and decided he would be Allen's "big brother." He gave Allen someone to talk to, someone to hang out with, and someone to protect him. He also served as an extra pair of eyes for Ann Iverson. If Tony caught his "little brother" doing something bad, he would turn Allen in. Sometimes Allen wanted to strangle Tony. Sometimes he wished he would just butt

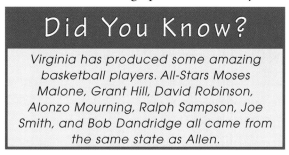

Did You Know?

Virginia has produced some amazing basketball players. All-Stars Moses Malone, Grant Hill, David Robinson, Alonzo Mourning, Ralph Sampson, Joe Smith, and Bob Dandridge all came from the same state as Allen.

The explosive speed NBA fans see on the basketball court helped Allen on the football field. Here he splits two tacklers during a high-school game.

out of his life. "I used to cry and scream at him," remembers Allen, "but he was doing it because he loved me and cared about me."

Allen managed to beat the odds and avoid serious trouble for 15 years. The same could not be said for the men in his life. Within a few months, both Tony and Michael were gone. Tony got into an argument with his girlfriend, the fight got out of hand, and she killed him. Then Michael, who had turned to drug-dealing to support the family, was caught by the police and sent to prison. The timing could not have been worse. Ann had just had her second daughter, Iesha, who was having severe health problems. Many frightening seizures and many trips to the doctor shook the emotions and frayed the finances in the Iverson home.

Allen felt overwhelmed. His concentration began to fade, his grades began to slip, and he stopped doing well in sports. For a time, he even stopped going to school. In short, he was giving up. Then, one day, something occurred to him. Like it or not, he was the "man" of the house. His family was now depending on him. He sat down, collected his thoughts, and began mapping out a plan. Allen wanted to become a pro athlete.

"My mom and my sisters, I just wanted to get them out of the projects so badly," he remembers. "I knew I had to succeed for them. People would say, 'Man, that's a million-to-one shot,' but I'd say, 'Not for me, it isn't.' I thought, for all the suffering they've done, they need to make it. They ought to have some satisfaction in life."

During Allen's second year at Bethel High, the medical bills finally caught up with his family and they were thrown out of their apartment. The cheapest deals in town were very far from the high school, and Ann did not want to add an extra 90 minutes to her son's travel time. Instead, she turned to a family friend named Gary Moore. Allen stayed with Moore for several months until Ann and the girls could get settled.

Moore coached youth football and had a good mind for the game. He talked to Allen about the finer points of football, and tried to make him understand the importance of discipline and consistency. It started, said Moore, with getting your homework done at night, waking up the next morning, having a decent breakfast, and getting to school on time. Allen moved back in with his mother, but Moore kept tabs on him and gave him an earful if he heard he was slipping.

Allen did slip from time to time. The pressures of survival made him edgy and angry. Sometimes in class he would snap at his teachers. Sometimes in practice, he would argue with a

Super moves and incredible speed made Allen an unstoppable kick returner.

Allen soars through the air for a dunk during his junior season at Bethel High.

coach. Sometimes he just skipped school and tried to sort everything out. There was never one specific incident anyone could point to, but over the next couple of years, people began to think of Allen as a "trouble-maker."

Of course, by the end of Allen's junior year, people also thought of him as the best two-sport athlete in the state. Allen was regularly mentioned among the nation's top high-school quarterbacks, and he was a great pass defender, too. He was named Virginia's top football player as a sophomore and again as a junior. In 1992 he led Bethel to the state championship. He passed for 201 yards in the title game, returned a punt for a 60-yard touchdown, and intercepted two passes.

On the basketball court, Allen set a state record with 948 points as a sophomore, and opened his junior year with a 37-point explosion. He had great moves, great vision, and a 40-inch (102-centimeter) vertical leap that propelled his 6-foot (183-centimeter) frame to the rim with stunning quickness. The college recruiters who came to watch him play believed he would be able to start as a freshman for any program in the country. Some said he was the best high-school point guard since Magic Johnson.

On the night of February 14, 1993, Allen's dreams nearly died. It was Valentine's Day, and he and some friends had arranged to meet at a local bowling alley to roll a few games and just kind of hang out. They were sent to a lane at the far end of the building, where their laughter and shouting would be less likely to disturb the other bowlers. Shortly after they got started, a group of young white men looked over and saw Allen making noise with his friends. Everyone in town knew who Allen was, and some resented how famous he had become.

Insults were hurled Allen's way. His friends shouted back. Soon the name-calling and trash-talking brought everyone nose-to-nose. The police were summoned, but by the time they arrived, a wild fight had broken out. Luckily, the officers were able to separate the combatants before anyone was seriously hurt. When they started asking who had done what, everyone said they remembered seeing Allen. One girl claimed he had hit her in the head with a folding chair. The funny thing was that Allen was nowhere to be found. To this day, he claims he left the premises as soon as the first punch was thrown. He wanted no part of this fight—not with his future on the line.

The Iverson File

ALLEN'S FAVORITE...

Book . . . . The Color Purple
Hobby . . . . Drawing
Charity . . . . Boys & Girls Clubs of America
Former Player . . . . . . Isiah Thomas
Current Player . . . . Latrell Sprewell— "I love his game."

"Football was my first love. That's what I thought I was going to do."

Believing he had fled the scene, the Hampton police tracked Allen down and arrested him. None of the white kids was charged with any crime. By the next morning, word had spread all over town: Allen Iverson was in jail.

"There are times I wish things could go back to the way they used to be, when nobody thought I was all that good. Seemed like there was a lot less to worry about then."

ALLEN IVERSON

Guilty as Charged

chapter }

"All I wanted to do was play basketball, and now I'm in the middle of this mess."

— ALLEN IVERSON

H ampton was not a happy place to be in 1993. The racial tension that had been bubbling beneath the surface for decades now exploded into words of hate and feelings of anger. Allen's arrest had divided the community, black against white, and the entire nation was watching. Every major news organization sent reporters to Hampton, hoping to find the truth behind the bizarre accusations that had put Allen in the spotlight. Tom Brokaw even anchored NBC's evening news broadcast from Hampton one night.

Allen was being charged with "maiming by a mob." Ironically, this law originally went on the books to protect black people from being beaten or lynched by groups of whites. Allen saw no irony in this situation. Although a prominent lawyer agreed to defend him for free and everyone was telling him he would be found not guilty, Allen knew that a guilty verdict—however unlikely—would carry serious jail time. He had

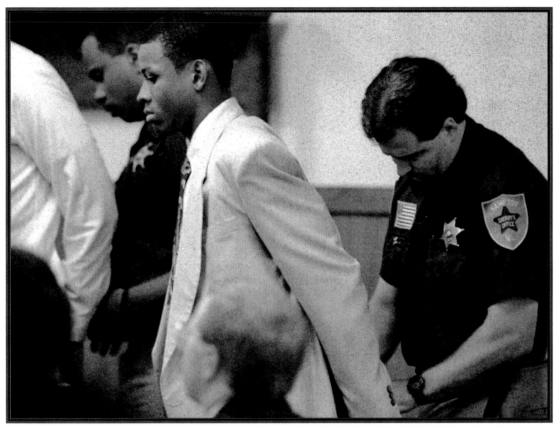

A dejected Allen is handcuffed after being found guilty.

already been thrown off the basketball team. If he missed his senior football season, no college in the country would come near him.

Allen's case went in front of Judge Nelson Overton in July. For two days, Allen listened to a series of witnesses who swore he was at the bowling alley, in the middle of the fight. His lawyer, Herbert Kelly Sr., instructed him to keep his mouth shut, no matter what he heard. It was the hardest thing Allen had ever done in his life. "I had to sit there and listen to people lie," he remembers sadly.

When the verdict came in, no one could believe it. Allen was found guilty. That August, at the hearing to determine his sentence, Judge Overton further shocked Allen and his supporters by handing down a five-year jail term. This was crazy! Even if Allen *had* been involved in the fight, he did not deserve such a harsh penalty. Allen just dropped his head. "Sometimes I wonder how everything got so messed up," he says.

Allen tried to relax and stay focused at the Newport News City Farm.
He refused to give up his dream of being a pro athlete.

In early September, while his classmates were beginning their senior year—and his teammates were starting the football season without him—Allen walked into the Newport News City Farm, a prison for young men. For someone used to being surrounded by friends, family, and fans, jail was almost unbearable. It was scary and lonely. Allen often just sat on his bed and wept. His lawyers had assured him that they would find a way to shorten his sentence and get him out. In the meantime, they said, he would have to be on his best behavior. Until then, all Allen had were his dreams. He clung to the hope that he could still become a successful professional athlete. No matter how grim things looked, he was determined to make it. "I had a big picture for my life," Allen explains. "I was not going to go back to the sewer."

Prison, however, had changed that picture. Allen knew that no college football coaches would be interested in him. Although rated among the country's top high-

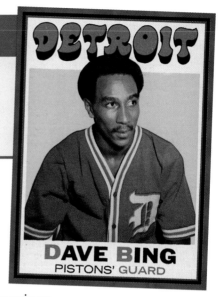

Did You Know?

By the time this card was printed in 1971, Dave Bing had established himself as a playmaking guard who could score at will. When he watched Allen play in high school, he saw a little bit of himself on the court—and a whole lot more. "I don't even know that he knows how quick he is," observed Bing.

DAVE BING
PISTONS' GUARD

school passers as a junior, he was going to miss his senior year, which is extremely important to the development of a young quarterback. So Allen turned to his second-best sport, basketball. To stay in shape, he shot baskets on the jail's rusted, rickety hoop. He imagined himself in game situations, and tried to work on the moves he would need to impress college recruiters.

Of course, to get a college scholarship, Allen would need a high-school diploma. Luckily, a tutor named Sue Lambiotte was able to visit him several times a week to help him study. She kept Allen focused and upbeat about his education. At Bethel High, he had kind of "cruised" through his classes. As the star of the school football, basketball, and baseball teams, Allen was not always forced to apply himself. But with Lambiotte, he worked hard.

In December 1993, Allen's lawyers convinced Virginia's governor, Douglas Wilder, that Allen had been jailed unfairly. Wilder agreed that the jury had convicted him without enough evidence, and granted him a pardon. Allen was free.

Everyone agreed that it would be a mistake to go back to Bethel High. So Allen continued working with Lambiotte to complete his education. To his surprise, she got even tougher. Allen was not allowed to miss a session, and his homework had to be done perfectly every night. They worked right through the summer, finishing both his junior and senior years. Lambiotte named him "class valedictorian" when he finished. Allen was proud of his accomplishment. Lambiotte admits that she was harder on him than on any other student. She jokes that his time studying with her was probably worse than jail.

Allen passed his final test on September 2, 1994. Less than a week later, he was off to college.

A Way Out

chapter 4

"He's going to be in a goldfish bowl."

— JOHN THOMPSON,
GEORGETOWN COACH

John Thompson is a basketball legend. A star center for Providence College in the early 1960s, he played in the NBA for two seasons as the backup for Bill Russell of the Boston Celtics. In 1972 he was hired to coach the Georgetown University team. When he began, Thompson was one of the few African-American coaches in Division I basketball. This helped him recruit some of the nation's top black high-school players to Georgetown. Thompson also developed a reputation for taking "troubled" kids and turning their lives around. When he retired, he had more than 500 victories to his credit.

After Allen was released from jail, his mother contacted Thompson. She told him that she believed he was the only coach who was right for

"He's a rabbit. He's just real, real quick."
KERRY KITTLES

John Thompson was more than Allen's coach. He sometimes acted as a substitute father.

Allen. She pleaded with him to bring her son to Georgetown. Thompson was flattered, but cautious. There was a secret to his success with young men no other coach would touch: If he thought a kid was bad, he would not recruit him; if he thought a kid was basically good—and serious about learning—he would take a chance. Thompson met with Allen and liked him. He looked at the facts surrounding Allen's case and knew that he had been unfairly treated. He told Allen if he got his diploma, he would give him a basketball scholarship.

As Allen packed his bags to head north to college, he was both excited and sad. He had gotten his life back on track—his dream was back within his reach. But he knew his mother and sisters would have to keep struggling while he was enjoying life at Georgetown, one of the richest and most prestigious universities in America. "That first day I left was one of the hardest in my life," Allen says. "It was one of the worst feeling I've ever had inside, knowing what my family was going through."

It had been almost two years since anyone had seen Allen playing against top competition on a basketball court. In the team's first few practices, he showed that he had not lost a step. In fact, he was now bigger, faster,

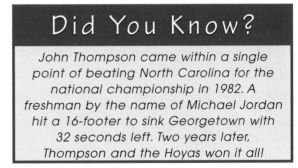

Did You Know?

John Thompson came within a single point of beating North Carolina for the national championship in 1982. A freshman by the name of Michael Jordan hit a 16-footer to sink Georgetown with 32 seconds left. Two years later, Thompson and the Hoyas won it all!

stronger, and smarter than he had been as a 17-year-old high-schooler. Allen could pick up his dribble 15 feet (4.6 meters) from the hoop, glide through the air, and slam the

All five Morgan State defenders surround Allen, who loses control of the ball. Learning to pass in these situations was a big step for him.

ball into the basket with amazing force. On defense, he could block anyone's shot, and sky past players 7 feet (213 centimeters) tall to pick rebounds off their fingertips. As the team's point guard, Allen was both energetic and creative. No one knew what he would do next, but they knew it might be something they had never seen before.

Coach Thompson had to determine how Allen would best fit in with the team. The Hoyas always had an excellent front line, and 1994–1995 was no exception. Don Reid, Jerome Williams, and Othella Harrington were good forwards, and a heavily recruited freshman named Jahidi White was ready to step right in at center. But in recent years, Georgetown had failed to come up with top-notch guards. Year after year, the Hoyas would hold their own in the paint, but get killed on the perimeter. If Georgetown's guards failed to shoot well from outside, opponents would collapse around Reid and Harrington and keep them from getting the ball, and the Hoya offense would stall. Going into the season, the plan was for George Butler, a good one-on-one player, to play the shooting-guard position. Allen and Eric Myles, both freshmen, would compete for the starting point-guard job.

At first, Coach Thompson leaned toward keeping Allen on the bench and starting Myles. But Allen had a way of changing the whole feel of a game when he was on the court. He was a special player, and the Hoyas would never be a special team if he was sitting down. Needless to say, Allen was happy with the decision to set him loose on the Big East. "I'm a creator," he smiles.

Georgetown's 1994–1995 season was one for the books. Fans remember it as "The Allen Iverson Show." Allen completely took over the team, racing up and down the court, making one highlight-reel play after another, and playing basketball at a speed that defied the laws of nature. It sometimes seemed as if he were trying to play every position at once; sometimes he did. Allen was everywhere, doing everything, all the time.

Unfortunately, four other players also happened to be wearing Georgetown uniforms, and they did not like Allen's game. On offense, he rarely passed the ball. On defense, he took chances that occasionally left his teammates trying to guard two people at once. Every so often, Allen's teammates would figure out what he was doing, and the Hoyas played like national champs. But just as often, they were out of sync, and looked like chumps.

The year did end on a high note. The Hoyas were invited to compete in the NCAA Tournament and did far better than expected. They played more team basketball, and won enough games to advance to the "Sweet 16." A loss to North Carolina ended their run, but all of the players were proud of their showing. Allen and his teammates could hardly wait for the next season to start.

Allen shakes a defender with a quick crossover and eyes the rim in a game against North Carolina.

Moving Forward, Pulling Back

chapter 5

*"If I wait, I think
good things will come."*
— **ALLEN IVERSON**

atience. During Allen's freshman year, it was a word he heard over and over again. But once he stepped on the basketball court, he seemed to forget its meaning. Allen replayed his first college season in his mind. He began to realize that a lot of the shots he took were bad ones, even though he thought he was going to make them at the time. Allen realized he had to change his approach to the game. Rather than forcing the action every time down the court, he needed to let plays develop. Then he could shoot, or drive, or pass the ball off.

"I'd pay to watch Allen play."
LAKERS COACH, PHIL JACKSON

Allen (number 6) poses with his teammates at the 1995 World University Games. Future NBA stars include Kerry Kittles (7), Ray Allen (8), and Tim Duncan (14).

During the summer of 1995, as a member of the team sent to compete at the World University Games in Japan, Allen got a chance to test out this new approach. Actually, he had little choice—everyone on the squad was a college star. Allen joined forces with his two greatest Big East rivals, Ray Allen of Connecticut and Kerry Kittles of Villanova, to win the gold medal. Also on this powerhouse squad were Othella Harrington and future NBA stars Tim Duncan and Austin Croshere.

A more mature and more patient Allen Iverson returned to Georgetown in the fall of 1995. He showed right away that he was ready to be a leader. In the Pre-Season National Invitation Tournament, he led the Hoyas all the way to the finals, against Arizona. But old habits die hard. In the Arizona game, Allen tried to do everything himself. Although he scored 40 points, no one else on Georgetown got more than 7, and the Hoyas lost, 91–81.

Allen continued to put up big numbers during the 1995–1996 season. But more often than not, they were the kind of numbers that helped his team win. Against Temple, he grabbed 10 rebounds—a very high number for a point guard. Against West Virginia, which double-teamed him all night, Allen found the open man again and

Allen became Georgetown's trusted floor leader during his sophomore season.

Allen celebrates Georgetown's 77–65 win over UConn in 1996.

again, finishing with 10 spectacular assists. Against Miami, he was a one-man defensive show, stealing 10 passes. And all the while, Allen was on pace to break the school scoring record.

What pleased John Thompson as much as his sophomore guard's amazing development was the fact that Harrington and Jerome Williams were finally thinking along with Allen. This trio terrorized Big East opponents all year long. As the season neared its conclusion, there was even talk of a trip to the NCAA Tournament's Final Four.

The biggest test of the year for Georgetown came in its second game against Connecticut. UConn, ranked third in the nation, had beaten the Hoyas five times in a row. Ray Allen, in his senior year with the Huskies, was being called the country's top player. UConn was good, but not *that* good. Ray was good, too, but not *that* good. In short, this was a game Allen Iverson wanted to have.

In the first half, Allen and the Hoyas played near-perfect basketball. Ray Allen scored just two points, and Georgetown was able to open up a good lead. In the second half, UConn tried to stay close but could not. Allen, who scored 26 points with six assists and eight steals, made the play of the game when he drove to the basket and stuffed the ball right right over Ray Allen. Georgetown won, 77–65.

The team's momentum continued right into the NCAA Tournament. The Hoyas defeated Mississippi Valley State, New Mexico, and Texas Tech to get within a single

college *stats*

SEASON	SCHOOL	SHOOTING %	ASSISTS/GAME	POINTS/GAME
1994–1995	Georgetown	39.0	4.5	20.4
1995–1996	Georgetown	48.0	4.7	25.0
Total		44.0	4.6	23.0

college *highlights*

Big East Defensive Player of the Year . . . . 1995 & 1996
School Record 926 points and 23.0 average 1996
All-Big East 1996
All-American 1996

win of the Final Four. But Massachusetts, led by All-American Marcus Camby, stopped Georgetown's run and ended its season. Despite the disappointment, Allen and his teammates were very proud. When the season-ending rankings were announced, the Hoyas were fourth. It was the school's highest national ranking during the 1990s.

Allen won every honor in sight for his tremendous sophomore season. Besides shattering the school records for points and scoring average, he was named to the All-America team. And for the second season, he was the Big East conference's Defensive Player of the Year. Allen was both proud and sad. He knew these achievements signaled that he was ready to fulfill his dream and become a professional player. But that would mean leaving Georgetown. Allen thought of the school as a second home. And Coach Thompson, in many ways, was like a father to him.

At the beginning of the season, the key to success for Allen was being able to wait and let things happen. Now, with a successful season under his belt, he could wait no longer. He announced he would leave Georgetown and enter the NBA Draft.

Allen answers questions during the press conference at which he announced he was leaving Georgetown for the NBA.

Philly Phanatic

chapter 6

"He's the fastest player I've seen enter the NBA in my 45 years."

— MARTY BLAKE, LEGENDARY PRO SCOUT

The Philadelphia 76ers had the first pick in the 1996 draft. The team's new owner, Pat Croce, was a young and energetic man who wanted the team to get a special player. The team was moving to a new arena, and Croce knew he had to have a star who could pack it every night. He needed someone who could electrify the crowd, someone with a big game and a big personality. He needed Allen Iverson.

Croce's staff advised against this move. Allen was barely 6 feet (183 centimeters) tall and weighed just over 150 pounds (61 kilograms). They were afraid he would not stand up to the punishment of the NBA. They were also afraid he

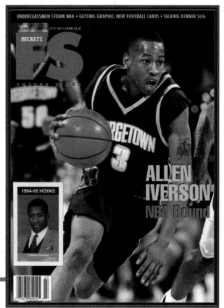

Allen's decision to turn pro put him on a lot of magazine covers in 1996.

*Philadelphia General Manager Brad Greenberg watches as Allen signs his
first pro contract with a quill pen provided by a Ben Franklin look-alike.
The 76ers made Allen feel like part of the city's great history.*

might self-destruct under the pressure of being a number-one pick. Croce knew he was
taking a chance. He knew Allen's confidence and aggressiveness might work against him
in the pros—both on and off the court—but he was willing to take a chance. On June
26, the Philadelphia 76ers made Allen the smallest player ever taken with the first pick in
the NBA Draft. "It meant a lot to me to go number one," says Allen. "I've been through
so many things in my life, so many obstacles."

When the regular season started, a sellout crowd watch Allen bury 12 of 19 shots
in a game against the Milwaukee Bucks. He played the game with joy and charisma and
intensity—something the team had lacked since the days of Charles Barkley. What the
experts found most interesting about his performance was how well his favorite move,
the crossover dribble, worked against the pros.

The crossover is a move Allen first tried on the playgrounds of Hampton, where one-on-one basketball is the name of the game. Allen would dribble the ball high, with his man positioned in front of him, watching Allen's head, shoulders, hips, and feet for a clue to his next move. Allen would then move his dribble in one direction, fake his man to that side, then with lightning quickness dribble the ball right in front of his body, pick up the dribble with his other hand, and explode in the opposite direction. The move takes about one-twentieth of the time it just took you to read about it. If you blink, you might miss it!

Allen used the crossover with limited success at Georgetown, because college teams are allowed to play zone defenses. Whenever Allen tried it, there was a second defender ready to meet him and stop his drive. But in the NBA, teams are not allowed to play zone defense. It is all about one-on-one. Within a couple of weeks, word got around that Allen had a move no one could stop. It is rare when a rookie brings a weapon to the league that works right away. It is almost unheard of for a weapon to create so much fear. The fear, of course, had to do with looking stupid. Players making millions of dollars a year do not like to

Allen drives to the hoop during his first NBA game.

> "Everywhere I went, people would shout Iverson! Iverson! Iverson! After a while I thought my name was Iverson."
>
> PAT CROCE

be stumbling over their feet while the rookie they are supposed to be guarding is dunking the ball 20 feet (6 meters) away. "The best is when I totally juke a guy," Allen laughs. "I can't stop to enjoy it, though—I've got a basket to score!"

As the season unfolded, coach Johnny Davis faced the same decision John Thompson had two years earlier. Do you try to tone down Allen's game and fit it into a system, or do you just let him play and hope his teammates learn to play along with him? Davis, once a slippery-fast guard himself, had found success as part of a strict offense with the Portland Trail Blazers. That team had won a championship, and Davis was a key contributor.

In the end, however, Davis realized that the old Trail Blazers had won because they had great players like Maurice Lucas and Bill Walton—not because Johnny Davis had been forced to play a conservative game. And when Davis looked down his bench, he did not see a lot of greatness. In fact, the 76ers had just one other quality NBA player, Jerry Stackhouse. And like Allen, he was most successful in the open court, not in a set offense.

Philadelphia played a lot of exciting basketball during the 1996–1997 season, and lost a lot of games. No one could stop Allen. Every time he got his hands on the ball, he tore up the court, looking for a scoring chance. If he was hot, he could score 40. If he was cold, it did not matter, he just kept shooting. Although this irritated his teammates from time to time, they liked Allen and admired his joy for the game. It made them remember how much fun basketball had been when they were kids. Between

Allen penetrates against the Kings' front line. He is not afraid to mix it up with the big guys.

games, Davis tried to teach Allen some of the tricks of the trade—the little things he would have to know in order to become a more complete player. According to the Philadelphia coach, Allen was eager to learn.

Not everyone was as thrilled with Allen as Coach Davis. Some of the league's veterans were angered by the amount of talking he did on the court. Allen adores a challenge, and he is a very vocal player. During a game with the Chicago Bulls, Michael Jordan got tired of Allen's "trash-talking" and advised him to show a little respect. Allen told Jordan that he respected no players once they set foot on the court. What Allen meant was that he has tremendous respect for the league's best players, but once the game begins, he will not give them a break just because they are superstars. "Once you step on the hardwood, if you over-respect someone, the battle's already been lost," he explains.

Make Your Point

Allen was the first Philadelphia 76er to become NBA Rookie of the Year—
and just the 7th point guard to win the award.

YEAR	PLAYER	TEAM	POINTS	ASSISTS
1961	Oscar Robertson	Royals*	30.5	9.7
1974	Ernie DiGregorio	Braves**	15.2	8.2
1979	Phil Ford	Kings	15.9	8.6
1988	Mark Jackson	Knicks	13.6	10.6
1995	Jason Kidd***	Mavericks	11.7	7.7
1996	Damon Stoudamire	Raptors	19.0	9.3
1997	Allen Iverson	76ers	23.5	7.5

*NOW SACRAMENTO KINGS** NOW L.A. CLIPPERS*** SHARED AWARD WITH GRANT HILL*

By the time this story made its way into the newspapers, however, it sounded like Allen was telling Jordan he had no respect for *him*. And in the NBA that is a big no-no. Soon the stories were saying that Allen had no respect for the game itself. One writer claimed that Allen was often late for practice, but he always showed up on time when Reebok needed him for an appearance. Allen had been signed to a multimillion-dollar deal by the sneaker company.

By the All-Star break, the controversy had only grown. As luck would have it, the NBA was honoring its 50 greatest players at the game, and Allen became a topic of conversation. When the

Did You Know?

All-time great Julius Erving said success was in the cards for Allen when he signed with the 76ers. "Philadelphia has an edge, and Allen's got an edge," observed Dr. J.

league's Hall of Famers were asked what they thought of Allen's remarks, they blasted him. Prior to the Rookies Game, when the players were being introduced, the fans let him have it, too. They booed even louder after the game, when he was awarded the MVP trophy.

Allen was embarrassed. He hated to look like a loud-mouthed punk in front of the game's legendary players. But most of all he could not believe people thought he took basketball for granted. Basketball had given him everything he had. Basketball had given him a second chance. Basketball had given him an education and rescued his family from the slums. "I have more love for this game than almost anyone," Allen says. "That's the only thing that hurts, that they think I have no respect for the game."

Of course, Allen had been through a lot worse. And although he was booed at every away game for the rest of the year, he knew the only thing he could do was play harder and better. If the fans wanted to boo him, fine. But he was determined to give 76er fans something to cheer about. During the month of April, Allen was almost unstoppable. He scored 40 or more points five straight times, and hit for a season-high 50 points against the Cleveland Cavaliers. Allen finished as the team leader in points, assists, and steals. And even though the press had raked him over the coals all season, when it came time to choose the NBA's Rookie of the Year, they had no choice but to give him the award.

Allen shows off his Rookie of the Year trophy. He became the first 76er to win the award.

New Man, New Plan

chapter 7

"I think God has sent me Larry Brown."
— ALLEN IVERSON

O n paper, the Philadelphia 76ers improved their record by four wins in Allen's first year. On the court, they had become much better than that. They now had the talent to beat any team on any night. It was simply a matter of adding the right pieces to complete the puzzle. To accomplish this task, the 76ers hired a new coach, Larry Brown. He is a miracle-worker when it comes to coach-

ing young players and struggling teams. He also has a very big ego. Brown expects players to do things his way.

Of course, Brown had never coached a player who could do the things Allen could.

Both men knew immediately that they would have to compromise.

Larry Brown and Pat Croce discuss the team's future during a practice.

Coach Brown urged Allen to pass first and shoot second—especially in situations like this!

During training camp, Allen did and said all of the right things. He knew he could benefit from Brown's coaching, and was aware of his reputation for turning ragtag teams into playoff contenders. For his part, Brown gave Allen the royal treatment. He knew talent when he saw it, and Allen's was off the charts. The 76ers were going nowhere if Allen was unhappy.

Still, all of the 76ers were expected to play by Brown's rules, including Allen. The first rule was that basketball is a team game. Brown explained to Allen that his job as a point guard was to get his teammates involved in the offense. That meant looking to pass first and shoot second. In the past, Allen had only given the ball up if he did not see a way to score. He felt that no one alive could guard him one-on-one. Brown told him that he would be even *more* effective if defenses were worried about guarding his four teammates. And the team would win more often. To prove his point, Brown showed Allen that on nights when he scored a lot of points, the team lost almost every time.

The 1997–1998 season saw the 76ers take a big step forward. Allen had his good nights and his bad nights. In a November game against the Rockets, he handed out 15 assists and did not turn the ball over once. A few games later, however, he took 17 shots and made only two. In January, Allen was spectacular in victories over the Lakers and

The addition of point guard Eric Snow (right) gave Allen a chance to move without the ball.

Bulls. But when he learned he was not voted into the NBA All-Star Game, he pouted for the rest of the month and the 76ers lost five straight. The joke around the league was that Allen should change his last name to "Me, Myself & Iverson." Allen needed to grow up, and needed to bring his "A Game" every single day, no matter what was going on in his life. That is what makes a good NBA player a great one.

Coach Brown was confident that Allen would continue to improve. He urged him to work harder on the weak points of his game, particular his outside shooting. He told Allen that this might mean coming to practice early and leaving late. To reach the next level, basketball had to be more than the most important thing in his life—it had to *be* his life. Allen was "the man" now. Brown had traded Jerry Stackhouse for shot-blocker Theo Ratliff. He had dealt away Jim Jackson and Clarence Weatherspoon, and decided to let Derrick Coleman go. If Allen did not take that next step, the team would be ruined.

Allen got the message. He spent the entire summer working on his outside shot. He sat and thought about how plays develop, and how he could create baskets by driving and passing instead of heaving up shot after shot. "I want to master this game," he says. "I want to know this game like Michael Jordan knows this game—not physically, but mentally."

Allen had plenty of time to think in the fall and winter of 1998. A labor dispute led to a lockout by the owners. They refused to start the season—or pay the players—until an agreement

Did You Know?

Allen's "posse"—which was made up of his old buddies from Hampton—was a major concern to the 76ers. The team asked him to cut loose his friends, but Allen did not want to be disloyal. "When I was struggling growing up, no running water in my house, the electric lights turned off, these were the guys who were with me," he explains. "They grew up with me. I'm not going to turn my back on them now."

Allen looks for the open man as he drives the baseline against towering Bo Outlaw.

was reached. For three months, no paychecks arrived. Like many NBA stars, Allen had an expensive lifestyle. He had a lot of friends and relatives who had come to depend on him for financial support. Michael Freeman, Allen's "father" for much of his childhood, was getting out of prison, and Allen had promised to support him completely until he got back on his feet. And Allen had a family of his own now, too. In 1995 he and his girlfriend, Tawanna Turner, had begun a family together. By 1998, there were two more mouths to feed—his daughter, Tiaura, and his son, Deuce (Allen Jr.). Allen had been smart about saving his money, so he was able to ride out this crisis. But it made him think hard about his growing responsibilities. "I'm a father, and my kids look up to me," he explains. "My kids have matured me, made me want to make better and smarter decisions, so I can set a good example for them."

The NBA settled its business, and the players returned to the court in February 1999 for a shortened, 50-game season. Among the new additions to the Philadelphia lineup were Matt Geiger, George Lynch, Tyrone Hill, and Harvey Grant—all talented individuals who had learned to play specific roles in the NBA. Also on the club was

The Orlando Magic planned to rough up Allen during the 1999 playoffs. As this photo shows, the strategy backfired.

Larry Hughes, a 20-year-old scorer picked up in the draft. The most interesting addition to the 76ers, however, was Eric Snow. Snow had been acquired in a trade midway through the previous season, and had impressed Brown with his playmaking ability. The Philadelphia coach decided to let Allen and Snow play together for long stretches. This relieved Allen of his point-guard duties, so he could create offense from the wings.

The strategy worked nicely. Opponents ended up guarding Snow with their point guard, and checking Allen with bigger, slower shooting guards. Allen started driving to the hoop and scoring points in bunches. When he did not have a high-percentage shot, he would kick the ball out to an open teammate. Free to move without the ball, Allen ran defenders into the ground. He could beat anyone in the NBA in a footrace, so imagine how easy it was to get open when he could run his man into a pick or lose him on the other side of a screen. At the end of the year, Allen was the NBA's scoring champion!

More important, the 76ers were now a winning team—a *playoff* team—for the first time since 1991. The 76ers beat the Orlando Magic and advanced to the second round of the playoffs, where they faced the Indiana Pacers. There was great excitement in Philadelphia. If the team could beat the Pacers, they would probably play the New York Knicks in the Eastern Conference Finals. And no one on the Knicks had been able to

Not even Allen's aggressive defense could prevent Reggie Miller from sinking the 76ers in four straight games.

contain Allen during the regular season. If the 76ers could slip past Indiana, they might find themselves playing for the NBA championship!

Unfortunately, Indiana's players seemed to be thinking the same thing. And in the NBA playoffs, you can never "look past" your opponent to a later series. The 76ers went down in four straight. Though disappointed by the sweep, Allen had plenty to be proud of. He was playing smarter, the team was playing better, and the city finally had a contender. Plus, he was the NBA scoring champ. But a taste of victory in the playoffs had whetted Allen's appetite for more. "A championship ring, that's the most important thing to me," he says. "Not the MVP or the scoring title. I'd rather have a championship."

Rising in the East

"Iverson will never have a better coach than Brown, and Brown will never have a better player."
— DAVE D'ALESSANDRO, SPORTSWRITER

Would the 1999–2000 season belong to the 76ers? It sure seemed that way. The NBA's Eastern Conference was "up for grabs," with no team having a clear advantage over the others. The Heat, Knicks, and Pacers were older and slower, and none of the other teams had the talent Philadelphia did. A lot would depend on Allen Iverson. Larry Brown had assembled a good team the year before, and they had learned to play together. He felt it was now up to Allen to mold his game to suit the team.

This was easier said than done. Injuries and inconsistent play made it hard for Allen to know who would be able to contribute from one night to the next. He was not sure how to "mold" himself under these circumstances. The 76ers were losing as often as they won. Coach Brown, frustrated by his players, tried to inspire them in different ways. He praised them, punished them, threatened them, and criticized them in the press. In Allen's case, he simply ignored him.

Allen and Larry Brown ignore each other during a 2000 practice.

Fine, Allen thought, if that is the way he wants to do, that is the way it will be. For a time, the two barely spoke. The other players did not know what to make of this strange relationship, and it threatened to destroy the team. Meanwhile, the 76ers continued to struggle, especially on offense. The team needed more scoring, but Brown did not want Allen to increase his shots. In fact, he already thought Allen was taking too many.

The solution was to make a trade. Young Larry Hughes, a great shooter, was not getting very many minutes as a backup guard. The decision was made to swap him for a forward who could score. This would take the pressure off Allen—and give him someone he could pass to when the team really needed a basket. What the 76ers got for Hughes was even better than they hoped: Toni Kukoc.

Kukoc was a perfect fit. He could shoot from anywhere on the court, but he was also an expert passer. With the Chicago Bulls, he had specialized in driving to the hoop, drawing a double-team, and then finding the man who had been left alone on the

Did You Know?

With the arrival of Toni Kukoc, Allen began moving without the ball. This worried opponents so much that they left the other Philadelphia players open for easy jumpers. "One of the things you have to learn is that you don't have to have the ball all the time to be effective," says Allen.

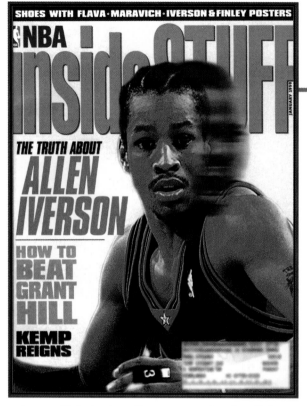

Is the NBA ready for a hip-hop superstar like Allen? Maybe not. The league was criticized by Allen's fans for "removing" some of his tattoos for this cover shot in January 1999.

perimeter. In short, Kukoc was the kind of player who could make everyone around him better.

The team suddenly became much more dangerous. When Kukoc spotted up from 20 feet (6 meters), the middle was wide open. When he drove, all sorts of room was created for open jumpers. Now when Allen got a pass, there was not always a defender right in his face. When he looked at the floor in front of him, he saw opportunities for himself and others that had not existed before. Allen's scoring went down slightly, but for every point he did not get, he made two or three terrific passes.

The rest of the season was a joy for the 76ers. Instead of worrying about how they would survive against their next opponent, they concentrated on playing their game as well as they could. If they played good defense, moved the ball around on offense, and executed their plays properly in the fourth quarter, they won. It did not matter whom they were playing.

Allen played the second half of the season with a painful toe injury. He claimed it did not hurt too much, but everyone on the team knew it did. Allen's defense and ball-handling were not affected, but his shooting clearly was. Luckily, Eric Snow had improved his shooting and was able to step up and drill key shots. And Philadelphia's defense had become almost impenetrable. Most important, Allen had become confident enough in his teammates not to force his shots. When other teams double-teamed him, he simply gave the ball up. Some nights he scored 30 or 40; others he was happy to get 15 or 20. The team was winning, and that was the important thing.

The 76ers finished the season 49–33. By playing so well through his injuries, Allen had become an inspiration both to his teammates and coach. They looked to him for leadership in the opening round of the playoffs, a best-of-five series against the Charlotte Hornets. As expected, the series was a tough one. As hoped, Allen stepped up and had a big game to open the series. He scored 40 and played great defense in a 92–82 win. The Hornets handled Allen well in Game 2, and forced the game into overtime. Derrick Coleman, now playing for Charlotte, scored eight points to put the game away and tie the series. But Philadelphia came right back and won Game 3. Allen, already nursing a broken toe and sore elbow, suffered a chip fracture in his right ankle during the game, and eventually had to go to the emergency room.

Allen took the floor for Game 4 limping and in extreme pain. In the second quarter, he reinjured his elbow, and hopped around waiting for the pain to go away. It did,

and he returned to score 26 points. The real story of this game, however, involved Aaron McKie, the backup point guard. Playing for Eric Snow (who also had a bad ankle), McKie broke open a tense game with four three-pointers in the fourth quarter. On several occasions, Allen was tempted to take shots, but decided instead to wait for the red-hot McKie to get open. These decisions may have meant the difference between winning and losing. And they did not go unnoticed by Allen's teammates, who praised him loudly after the game.

Philadelphia's next opponent was Indiana. The 76ers were banged-up, but still felt they could take

Allen clutches his elbow during Game 4 of the Charlotte series. He shook off the pain and scored 26 points.

A tearful Allen is comforted by his mother as the final seconds tick away on the 1999–2000 season.

the Pacers. Unfortunately, Indiana was ready. Reggie Miller scored 16 points in the first quarter, then rained three-pointers on Philadelphia after it had battled back to make the game close in the final quarter. Game 2 was not much better, as Jalen Rose scored 30 and the Pacers cruised to an easy win. And Game 3 was a disaster, as Indiana scored 32 of the final 48 points to win by eight. There were a lot of reasons for the team's poor showing. Allen was hurting, Kukoc shot poorly and played bad defense, Snow tried to play through his injury but could not.

As Philadelphia fans prepared themselves for another sweep by the Pacers, something amazing happened. In Game 4, Tyrone Hill played the game of his life, the emotional Miller was ejected for fighting with Matt Geiger, and six 76ers scored in double figures. The result was a hair-raising 92–90 win. In Game 5, Theo Ratliff caught fire and Allen came alive with 37 points in a 107–86 blowout. Could it be? Could the 76ers pull off the impossible?

Sadly, the team's dramatic comeback ended in Game 6. No team in NBA history had ever erased a 3–0 deficit to win a playoff series, and Philadelphia was not quite up to making history. Allen fought the good fight, trying to ignore the pain in his elbow, ankle, and toe, but the Indiana defense was just too good and the Pacers won 106–90. As the final seconds ticked away, Allen sat on the bench and cried.

"I have to get better," he says, "and we have to get better as a team. I'm a competitor, and as the clock went down, I saw my whole season pass by, just like that. It hurt."

The Final Ingredient

"Obviously, Allen's our leader on the court. Off the court is where he had to get better, and he's improving. We're looking to him more, and he's realizing the effect he can have on us."

— TEAMMATE MATT GEIGER

When Allen Iverson came into the NBA, everyone—Allen included—agreed that he had a lot to learn. Players may be born with the gifts to achieve greatness, but great players are not born, they are made. Since 1996, Allen has added valuable experience to his tremendous talents. He is on the verge of becoming a great player.

The final ingredient, some say, is still missing. For a team to fulfill its destiny, its best player must also be its leader, and in the NBA that means being the wisest, most dedicated, and most consistent player on the court. Allen

Ann Iverson is never hard to spot at her son's games.

#3
My #1
Son!!

pro stats

SEASON	TEAM	SHOOTING %	STEALS/GAME	ASSISTS/GAME	POINTS/GAME
1996–1997	76ers	41.6	2.1	7.5	23.5
1997–1998	76ers	46.1	2.2	6.2	22.0
1998–1999	76ers	41.2	2.3	4.6	26.8*
1999–2000	76ers	40.8	2.1	4.7	28.4**
Total		42.8	2.1	5.9	24.9

• LED NBA   ** SECOND IN NBA

pro highlights

#1 Overall Pick, NBA Draft	1996
MVP of NBA Rookie Game	1997
NBA Rookie of the Year	1997
NBA Scoring Champion	1999
First-Team All-NBA	1999
Playoff Record 10 Steals in a Game	1999
High Scorer in All-Star Game	2000
Second-Team All-NBA	2000
NBA All-Star	2000

is close, but he is not there yet. The good news is that Allen clearly understands what is involved in taking that next giant step.

After the 2000 season, he sought advice from the great Magic Johnson. Like Allen, Magic could do it all. Allen asked him what his next move should be. Magic said that being a leader starts with what you do when there are no fans or television cameras around. It begins with practice—getting there early, working on your weaknesses, showing your teammates that even the best players can get better. It also means playing as hard in scrimmages as you would in a game—which makes your teammates work harder, and makes them better. And it means staying after practice to work with other players, or talk with coaches, or chat with reporters about the team, not just about yourself.

Allen listened intently to every word. Money, fame, awards—he has all these things. What he does not have is a championship ring. Magic? He won four. Something Magic did *not* say—but Allen picked up on—was that he *hated* to lose. Nothing made him feel emptier than a loss, no matter how well he had played. Larry Brown began to see this in Allen during the playoffs. Perhaps that is why, when Brown was offered a dreamy coaching job at his alma mater, the University of North Carolina, he turned it down to stay with the 76ers.

Allen has been letting his friends and teammates know that they will be seeing a different person in the coming seasons. He will continue to play with the same fire and intensity. He will still trash-talk and he will even butt heads with his coach from time to time.

The same people who booed Allen as a rookie now strain for high fives when he leaves the court. Winning over the fans is just one of the steps involved in achieving superstar status.

But everything he does will be keenly focused on one thing: Doing whatever it takes to make his team into a winner.

"I haven't played the game I want to play yet," says Allen. "I want to be unstoppable—in every fashion. Years from now, when people are talking about Magic and Michael, I want my name to be mentioned, too."

Index